BUS OPERATORS 1970
South-West and Southern England

Gavin Booth

Ian Allan
PUBLISHING

Contents

Introduction	3
South-West and Southern England Snapshot	4
Setting the scene	5
South Central England	9
West of England	41
Bristol and Gloucestershire	65

First published 2006

ISBN (10) 0 7110 3034 0
ISBN (13) 978 0 7110 3034 3

All rights reserved. No part of this book may be reproduced or transmitted in any form or by any means, electronic or mechanical, including photocopying, recording or by and information storage and retrieval system, without permission from the Publisher in writing.

© Ian Allan Publishing Ltd 2006

Design by Hieroglyph

Published by Ian Allan Publishing

An imprint of Ian Allan Publishing Ltd, Terminal House, Station Approach, Shepperton, Surrey TW17 8AS

Printed by Ian Allan Printing Ltd, Riverdene Business Park, Molesey Road, Hersham, Surrey KT12 4RG

Code: 0604/C

Visit the Ian Allan Publishing wesbite at www.ianallanpublishing.com

Front cover: Green-painted Bristol/ECW products abounded in the area covered by this book. In the north of the area, in Gloucester in 1970 is a 1961 FSF6G with 60-seat forward entrance body in the Bristol Omnibus Company's Gloucester City fleet.
Tony Wilson

Back cover, upper: King Alfred of Winchester had an esoteric taste in new buses, like this 1964 AEC Renown with 75-seat Park Royal body, seen in Winchester Broadway in the final days of the company's independence, in 1973. The bus passed with the company to Hants & Dorset that year.
Ted Jones

Back cover, lower: Southampton Corporation built up a substantial fleet of East Lancs-bodied Leyland Atlanteans in the 1960s and 1970s. This is a 1969 PDR1A/1 example in the autumn sun at Hedge End in October 1969.
Ted Jones

Previous page: Much of the territory covered by this book was deeply rural, typified by this May 1970 view at Woodgreen, Dorset, with a 1954 Wilts & Dorset Bristol LS5G with Eastern Coach Works (ECW) 41-seat body.
Martin Llewellyn

This page: Former Tilling Group companies, now grouped with former BET Group companies under the recently-created National Bus Company, dominated south-west England, and this Wilts & Dorset Bristol RELL6G with dual-door ECW body, was typical of new buses delivered during 1970.
M A Penn

Facing page: There were few significant independent operators in the area. Best known was King Alfred of Winchester whose 1970 deliveries included three of these Leyland Panther PSUR1A/1R with 52-seat Plaxton bodies. In 1973 King Alfred sold out to Hants & Dorset.
G J Wadley

Introduction

The changes to the British bus industry in the period around 1970 affected different areas in different ways. The first book in this series covered the south-east and Eastern Counties of England, where arguably the most significant changes affected London Transport, which in 1970 lost its Country Area operations to the London Country company, itself a child of the recently-created National Bus Company. The second book covered Scotland and north-east England. In Scotland the most visible reminder of the creation of the Scottish Transport Group was the gradual disappearance of the former David MacBrayne bus network into the established Scottish Bus Group companies; in the north-east it was the establishment of Tyneside PTE, which would have an increasing influence on bus services on Tyneside and Wearside over the succeeding years.

In south-west England the creation of National Bus Company was making itself felt, both through the rationalisation of companies and territory that was taking place, and by the sale of one of the municipal operations to NBC.

This book continues west from the south-east book, covering the counties of Hampshire, Wiltshire, Dorset, Somerset, Devon, Cornwall, and Gloucestershire.

This beautiful corner of England witnessed some of the earliest motorbus services and in 1970 was home to five municipal operations – though one would last just three months into the year – and several major NBC subsidiaries, all but one descended from the former Tilling Group, balancing the domination of the former BET Group further east along the south coast.

Although it has major regional centres like Bristol, Plymouth and Southampton, and significant historic centres like Bath, Cheltenham and Salisbury, this is an area with a low population density, and this affects the provision and profitability of bus services.

History and geography both played their part in the pattern of bus services in the south-west in 1970, and by the 21st century the difficulty of providing viable services in some areas had created huge problems for both operators and passengers.

Back in 1970, though, there were few indications of the traumas that would come. Big state-owned companies were running big buses on a well-established network of routes, and this is the world that is captured in this book. ∎

Gavin Booth
Edinburgh

South-West and Southern England Snapshot

The south-west as defined for this book is a very varied area, never far from the coast, where the economy relied heavily on agriculture, fishing and forestry, supplemented by a thriving, but largely seasonal, tourist industry with pockets of heavier industry particularly around Bristol and Southampton.

Tourism was important for the bus operators, but the face of tourism was changing. There was still the traditional summer fortnight by the sea at places like Bournemouth, Torbay, North Devon and Weston-super-Mare, but by 1970 Britons were beginning to succumb to the allure of cheaper flights to the sun, and seaside resorts, even in the sunny south-west, were beginning to notice a change in visitor patterns. Car-borne tourism was increasing too, affecting the viability of coach services like the famous Royal Blue and Associated Motorways networks.

After decades when the population of much of the south-west was in decline or showing modest growth there were signs that numbers were increasing in several areas, partly as people moved away from more congested areas to retire, and partly because of the growth of leisure and other service industries.

Access to the area has always been good, with mainline rail services from London to the Bristol area, to Exeter, Plymouth and Cornwall, and to Southampton, Bournemouth and the Isle of Wight. Main road access too was improving, and this allowed coach operators to accelerate journey times, which helped them to be more competitive.

The problem was often the difficulty of reaching smaller towns and villages away from the main centres of population. These places had benefited from the existence of large network operators who were able to cross-subsidise services that could never hope to be remunerative with the profits earned from the town and city networks and the interurban trunk routes. Under the old Tilling and BET group regimes this type of cross-subsidy was largely accepted as a fact of life when you were providing a public service, but with Tilling and BET now together, slightly uncomfortably, in the recently-created National Bus Company, the people at the top were under pressure from the Treasury to make realistic financial returns, and these marginal services were increasingly coming under the microscope, starting a process that continues to this day, with network operators withdrawing from unremunerative routes, leaving the local authority to pick up the pieces if the services are judged to be socially necessary. This has attracted lower-cost local operators into the market and the south-west scene today is very different from that of 1970.

But back then it was still the big players that dominated the scene. The Tilling Group companies had often been found in the more rural areas and seemed to be most comfortable with a mix of rural, urban and interurban work. The BET Group companies often had tramway ancestry, so were found in the more industrial areas, though in southern England operators like East Kent and Southdown, and in the south-west, Devon General, thrived on a diet that mixed urban and rural work.

Bristol was in many ways an exception. As one of England's major cities, it was unusual that its bus services were provided not by the local council but by an important company operator; the reasons for this are explained in the book. Municipal bus operation thrived at Bournemouth, Plymouth, Southampton and Swindon, while in Exeter the local council decided to sell out to NBC during 1970. There were small pockets of independent operation, but already one of the famous names, Silver Star, had sold out to the local territorial operator and another, King Alfred, would follow in 1973. ∎

Exeter sold its corporation bus operation to Devon General in 1970, bringing some decidedly municipal types into NBC hands, like this 1958 Leyland Titan PD2/40 with Weymann body and 1960 Massey-bodied Guy Arab IV.
Martin Llewellyn

Setting the scene

In 1970 the British bus industry was at the crossroads. It had enjoyed boom years after World War 2 and had arguably reacted too slowly to the huge social changes that coincided with the 'New Elizabethan' age of the early 1950s. The steady growth of private motoring and the widespread purchase of television sets are normally blamed for the apparently unstoppable decline in passenger numbers and there is certainly a lot of truth in this. Although new motorcars were still relatively expensive, congestion was unheard of in many parts of the country and motoring still had a romantic appeal. Television was more accessible, and became an essential fixture in many houses, particularly after the launch of Independent Television in 1955 offered an alternative to the single BBC channel. Television, of course, affected bus patronage because increasingly people stayed in to watch 'the box' where previously they would have visited cinemas and theatres in the evening. It could be argued that, like the bus industry, cinemas and theatres were slow to respond to the television threat, although like today's bus industry, cinemas and theatres have reinvented themselves in new ways that appeal to wider audiences.

But in 1970 those changes in fortune had still to come and for the bus industry things looked fairly bleak. In 1954 buses had accounted for 38 per cent of passenger transport, with railways on 18 per cent and private motoring on 35 per cent. In 1970 that had all changed. Private motoring represented 76 per cent, expressed in passenger kilometres, with buses and coaches down to 14 per cent and railways to 9 per cent.

In some quarters one way forward was seen as making economies of scale by creating larger units. In four conurbations – Birmingham, Liverpool, Manchester and Newcastle – the answer was to create Passenger Transport Authorities that would mop up at least the local municipal bus operations and bring them together under centralised control. In 1969/70 the first four PTAs were set up, deciding policy and working through the Passenger Transport Executives, the PTEs. Twenty municipal bus operators disappeared into the first round of PTEs and a second set of PTEs were set up a few years later in Scotland and Yorkshire.

The PTEs accounted for over 6,000 of the UK parc of 74,000 buses. Add London Transport's 6,000-plus buses, and the 12,000 buses remaining in municipal ownership and you quickly realise how many buses were in public ownership. And that's before you add in the two big state-owned groups which could field another 26,000 buses. Add them all together and it will be seen that two in every three buses in the UK were publicly owned.

The two big state-owned groups were National Bus Company and Scottish Transport Group, both set up at the start of 1969. NBC was the monolith set up to weld together the two groups that had dominated England and Wales for more than 30 years. The Tilling Group had been state-owned since 1948 and had companies operating at the Scottish border and at Land's End and a patchwork quilt of subsidiaries in-between. The British Electric Traction Group, BET, had an equally significant patchwork coverage and was particularly strong in largely

Southampton was one of the four municipal fleets remaining in the area after Exeter sold out. Here the old and new orders are represented as a 1967 AEC Regent V/Neepsend passes between two 1971 Leyland Atlantean/East Lancs.
Royston Morgan

industrial areas like Lancashire, Yorkshire, South Wales, the Midlands and south-east England; Tilling's strengths were often in more rural areas, like north-east England, East Anglia, North Wales and the south-west. The privately-owned BET Group decided in 1968 to sell its UK bus interests to the state, paving the way for the creation of NBC.

The Scottish Transport Group had brought together the state-owned Scottish Bus Group with state-owned shipping interests. Although STG and the PTEs played no part in the 1970 south-west bus scene, NBC was a significant player and the area saw some of the earliest reorganisations that would become a regular feature during NBC's history.

1970 was also a crossroads for bus design. With buses expected to complete 12-15 years in service with their original owners, and often more, there were still plenty of buses around that were conceived in the early 1950s and which were increasingly unsuited to an industry that was trying to trim its sails by dispensing with conductors and moving to more driver-only operation. The early underfloor-engined single-deckers were certainly suitable as driver-only buses, as indeed were a number of the contemporary front-engined single-deckers that were converted as a stopgap measure. But front-engined double-deckers were more of a problem. Rear-entrance types were clearly out of the question but the forward-entrance types that gained in popularity from the late 1950s were suitable, if hardly ideal, and the front-entrance rear-engined types from the same time were preferred.

The trouble was, it was 1966 before driver-only double-deckers were legalised, and many operators were impatient to economise by cutting the wages bill. Before 1966 many had invested in full-size single-deckers, many of which could carry almost as many seated passengers as the old lowbridge double-deckers they were replacing. 'Full-size' from 1961 was 36ft, and while some operators switched back to double-deckers after 1966, others stuck with single-deckers and started a gradual process where the proportion of double-deckers has gradually fallen.

The municipal, independent and BET fleets had a fairly free hand in vehicle purchase. There had been a wide range of models from a variety of manufacturers in the 1950s but the range of models and manufacturers declined in the 1960s as the industry embarked on a series of acquisitions and mergers that would see British Leyland as the dominant bus builder in the UK at a time when the vast majority of the country's buses and coaches were UK-built, and the importers, particularly from Northern Europe, had yet to make any impact.

One consequence of British Leyland's near-monopoly situation would be a dramatic reduction in choice, but in 1970 this was still to come. Leyland, and its new-found stablemates at AEC, Bristol, Daimler and Guy, offered single-deck bus and coach chassis and a reducing range of double-deck chassis. The reason for the reduction was the decision to drop long-running models like the AEC Regent V, Bristol Lodekka, Daimler CV, Guy Arab and Leyland Titan, which were sacrificed in the name of the government's Bus Grant scheme which gave operators a quarter of the cost of new buses meeting certain stipulations – essentially that they were suitable for driver-only operation; the subsidy would rise to half the cost before it was dropped.

Bus Grant prompted a feeding frenzy among operators and undoubtedly helped operators to modernise their fleets as well as giving the manufacturing industry a welcome boost. The trouble was, the manufacturing industry at the time was largely Leyland, and some operators were becoming distinctly uneasy about Leyland's near-monopoly and the effect this had on customer choice and, skewed by the Bus Grant scheme, new vehicle prices. This uncertainty prompted various manufacturers to dip a toe in the UK market, notably Scania working

On the Isle of Wight, Southern Vectis was another former Tilling company whose fleet reflected Tilling's standardised approach. This is a 1969 Bristol RESL6G with 43-seat ECW body.
Edward Shirras

Above: Devon General was the only major BET Group company in the south-west and in 1971 control of the company would pass to its neighbour, the former Tilling company, Western National. This brought an end to Devon General's fondness for AEC chassis, and this 1971 Reliance 6MU3R with 41-seat Willowbrook body, would be one of the last AECs delivered to the fleet.
Edward Shirras

Left: In 1967 20 of these Bristol Lodekka FSF6G were transferred from Bristol Omnibus to neighbouring Western National, in exchange for bigger FLF types, but they would return in 1970 following a redrawing of company areas. This one is at Paignton in 1968.
W T Cansick

with MCW, which would shortly be joined by Volvo and DAF. MCW moved on from the Scania relationship to build its own buses, but another UK builder that saw an opportunity was Seddon, which played its part throughout the 1970s. And always there in the background were Bedford and Ford, American-owned but building bus and coach models in the UK; although their chassis had traditionally been bodied as coaches, saving weight was seen as another means of saving money, particularly on more marginal routes, and some major operators invested heavily in lighter-weight types.

Choice would be further restricted following the 1970 introduction of the Leyland National, a single-deck citybus developed jointly by the two biggest players in the business, British Leyland and NBC. Designed for mass production, it was perhaps inevitable that British Leyland would help its chances in the market by withdrawing any model that might be seen to compete, so out went the largely unloved AEC Swift, Daimler Roadliner and Leyland Panther, as well as the universally admired Bristol RE, leaving operators with virtually no choice when it came to rear-engined single-deck buses. The fact that the Leyland National was conceived as a complete bus alarmed bodybuilders who had made a good living out of bodying single-deck buses. Some were already part of the British Leyland empire – Eastern Coach Works, Park Royal and Roe – but others like Alexander, East Lancs, Marshall, MCW, Northern Counties and Willowbrook were more vulnerable, particularly firms like Marshall and Willowbrook that majored on single-deck bodies.

British Leyland would pursue a similar policy with its double-deck range, though it encountered more opposition, and by this time there were viable competitors available. That was in the future, though. In 1970 you could buy a Bristol VRT, Daimler Fleetline or Leyland Atlantean double-decker, or a range of single-deckers; the Swift, RE and Panther were still available, just, and the mid-engined AEC Reliance and Leyland Leopard were available, along with the rear-engined Seddon RU and front-engined Bedford and Ford models. A taste of things to come was provided by the Metro-Scania, a single-deck citybus that was the result of a liaison between MCW and Scania. It sold in respectable quantities for a short time, and no doubt gave British Leyland a few sleepless nights, but never came near to challenging Leyland's National offering.

The events around 1970 in the UK bus-operating and manufacturing industries would lead to a certain amount of stability, but this would be short-lived when the political powerbase changed and the bus industry edged towards its greatest shake-up for half a century. If northing else, the changes around 1970 gave the industry a bit of breathing-space, and arguably meant that it was in better shape to face the uncertainties that were to come. ∎

An independent survivor in Somerset was Hutchings & Cornelius of South Petherton, whose famous Dennis Loline/East Lancs is seen in Yeovil in 1970.
Chris Aston/Omnicolour

South Central England

For many bus enthusiasts of a certain age the geography of Britain was defined by the Ian Allan British Bus Fleets series of 'ABC' pocket books produced in the 1950s and 1960s. Some areas were clear-cut – like Scotland, Lancashire and East Anglia. But along the south coast of England there was an area described as South Central, a term that covered bus operators that couldn't be described as South East, but weren't quite in the West of England. Most of these are covered in this book, but Reading Corporation and Thames Valley were covered in the book covering the south-east, and City of Oxford will be in the book that covers the Midlands. For the purpose of this series, the South East ended at the Solent with Portsmouth Corporation, Provincial and Southdown, so our South Central starts there and takes in major territorial companies like Hants & Dorset, Wilts & Dorset, as well as Southern Vectis, and the municipal fleets at Bournemouth, Southampton and Swindon.

Hants & Dorset Motor Services Ltd was by far the largest operator in the area with, in 1970, some 799 buses in its fleet. Those 799 buses were strictly spread between the Hants & Dorset and Wilts & Dorset fleets, two fellow Tilling Group companies that had in 1964 been merged under Hants & Dorset management. Although in 1970 their buses still wore separate liveries – green/cream for Hants & Dorset and red/cream for Wilts & Dorset – and carried their own fleetnames, they shared a registered office in Bournemouth, and would under National Bus Company become simply Hants & Dorset, with red-painted buses.

Redrawn county boundaries meant that Bournemouth, in Hampshire in 1970, would 'move' to Dorset in 1974.

Hants & Dorset had its roots in Bournemouth & District Motor Services in 1916, which in 1920 was retitled with the Hants & Dorset name, under the control of Tilling and BAT (TBAT). The company expanded throughout the counties featured in its name and gained access to Southampton in 1930.

Above: Hants & Dorset's large fleet of Bristol K types was disappearing fast in 1970. This ECW-bodied 55-seat lowbridge KS6B example, new in 1950, sits in the sun at Bournemouth bus station.
Omnicolour

Left: Hants & Dorset's Bristol Ks were followed from 1954 by Lodekkas. In October 1969, a 1954 LD6G 58-seater is seen at Fareham. It features the earlier style of front grille.
Ted Jones

Like so many of the companies that survived into recent times, H&D expanded by acquisition and agreements with other operators. An important agreement had been reached in 1924 with Elliott Brothers, the long-established coach company, also Bournemouth-based, which operated under the Royal Blue banner. H&D agreed not to operate excursions, tours or long-distance coach services from Bournemouth and Royal Blue's local bus services passed to H&D. In 1935 Southern and Western National bought Elliott Bros, retaining the profitable long-distance coach business and passing the excursion, tour and private hire business to H&D.

Poole Corporation abandoned its tramway system in 1934 and H&D provided replacement bus services, giving it a stronghold in that town.

From 1929 half of the share capital in H&D was held by the Southern Railway, and when the Tilling and BAT interests were reallocated in 1942, the BAT interest in H&D passed to Tilling, which meant that the company passed into state control in 1948 as part of the Tilling Group within the British Transport Commission.

Wilts & Dorset began running buses in 1915, between Salisbury and Amesbury and in 1921 bought the Salisbury & District company. In 1931 it came under the control of TBAT and the Southern Railway. Twenty years later in 1951 it took responsibility for Red & White's 54-vehicle Venture subsidiary, based in Basingstoke, an important acquisition when Basingstoke was developed as one of the second generation New Towns, catering for London overspill residents.

In 1963 W&D acquired the well-known independent, Silver Star of Porton Down and this reinforced its strong position in the Salisbury area. Although in 1964 management of W&D was passed to Hants & Dorset, it retained its separate identity for a number of years.

In 1966 H&D's masters, the Transport Holding

Above: After several years on frontline coaching duties, Hants & Dorset rebuilt several of its 1962/63 vintage Bristol MW6G coaches with ECW bodies for driver-only operation. In the conversion they gained roof-mounted destination boxes and folding doors.
J G Carroll

Left: In 1967 Hants & Dorset bought five Bedford VAM14s with locally-built Strachans dual-door standee bodywork with seats for 33 passengers and standing space for 25 more. This one is seen in Westover Road, Bournemouth.
B W Spencer

Left: **Bound for Fareham, a smartly-presented Hants & Dorset Bristol FS6G Lodekka with 60-seat ECW body.**
Kevin Lane collection

Below: **Another of Hants & Dorset's 1961 Bristol FS6G Lodekkas, fitted with platform doors.**
Kevin Lane collection

Devizes, Marlborough, Shaftesbury, Warminster and Winchester. To the south, west and north W&D was surrounded by other former Tilling Group companies – Hants & Dorset, Southern/Western National, Bristol Omnibus, Thames Valley – and its eastern boundary was with the former BET Group fleet, Aldershot & District. W&D's principal routes included long trunk services from Salisbury to Andover, Devizes, Marlborough, Trowbridge and Weymouth, services between Andover and Basingstoke and Newbury, and between Basingstoke and Newbury.

The joint Hants & Dorset/Wilts & Dorset fleet in 1970 consisted of 799 vehicles, mostly Eastern Coach Works-bodied Bristols, but with variety added by some recent deliveries as well as buses taken over from Silver Star. In 1970 NBC acquired the formerly independent Gosport & Fareham Omnibus company, trading as Provincial, and although its private hire and contract work was transferred to H&D and its registered office was transferred to H&D's at Bournemouth, it remained a separate legal entity.

Company, acquired Bournemouth-based Shamrock & Rambler Motor Coaches and the company's Hampshire operations passed to H&D.

Hants & Dorset's traditional operating area ran along the south coast from Portsmouth west to Swanage with fellow NBC companies Southdown to the east, Southern National to the west, and Wilts & Dorset to the north. Its main towns were Bournemouth, Lymington, Poole, Southampton, Swanage and Winchester, and its most frequent routes from Bournemouth served Lymington, Salisbury and Swanage, and from Southampton served Lymington and Winchester. H&D had garages at Bournemouth, Eastleigh, Fareham, Lymington, Poole, Ringwood, Southampton, Winchester and Woolston, with its central works at Southampton.

Wilts & Dorset's area was centred on Salisbury and included quite a number of 'border' towns where its operating area met those of other NBC companies – places like Basingstoke,

The oldest buses in the combined fleet in 1970 were Bristol K6As with heavily rebuilt open-top bodies; the chassis dated from 1945 and the bodies from 1937. Otherwise there were 20-year-old LL type single-deckers, and these would be withdrawn in the course of the year along with K6B and KS6B double-deckers of the same vintage. Also withdrawn were the open-top Bristol K6As dating from 1944, though four slightly newer K5Gs survived.

The rest of the fleet was a typical Tilling mix of Bristol/ECW standard types. There were the underfloor-engined LS buses and coaches, MW coaches, and a growing fleet of the current LH and RELL types. Double-deckers were principally Bristol Lodekkas of the LD, FS and FLF types.

Although most Tilling Group companies had survived on a strict diet of Bristol/ECW products for at least 20 years, there were indications of a more liberal attitude to vehicle purchase in vehicles like the Strachans-bodied Bedford VAM14s bought in 1967 and Willowbrook-bodied VAM70s in 1968. Although

Left: A 1956 Hants & Dorset Bristol LD6G in service in Southampton late in 1969.
Ted Jones

Below: In the early days of National Bus Company at Bournemouth bus station is a 1957 Hants & Dorset Lodekka LD6G 60-seater.
Omnicolour

Below: Heading out of Southampton for Moorgreen in October 1969, a 1959 LD6B Lodekka. Like the other H&D double-deckers it sports the distinctive sun visor over the driver's windscreen.
Ted Jones

Left: A later photo of Hants & Dorset Lodekkas sporting the NBC corporate fleetnames in Southampton. Prominent is a 1957 LD6G.
Tony Wilson

Centre: Representing Hants & Dorset's longer forward-entrance Lodekkas, a 1966 FLF6G 70-seater in Southampton in June 1968.
Tony Wilson

Below: In suburban Southampton in 1968, a 1957 Hants & Dorset Bristol LS5G with 43-seat ECW bus body.
Tony Wilson

lightweights, these had two-door bodies, as did contemporary Bristol LHs; the dual doorway layout with a separate central exit was briefly fashionable as driver-only operation spread but most operators outside major cities quickly reverted to a single door at the front.

Other non-standard types in the combined H&D/W&D fleet included AEC Reliances that had been absorbed into the H&D fleet from the Shamrock & Rambler business, and Duple-bodied Bedford coaches, including three-axle VAL70s. This trend would continue as Wilts & Dorset received three more Duple-bodied VAL70s in 1970. An interesting 1970 delivery to Hants & Dorset was a Plaxton-bodied Leyland Leopard, the first Leyland in the fleet for many years.

New bus deliveries to H&D/W&D in 1970 were Bristol RELL6Gs with 45-seat two-door ECW bodies, and Bristol LH6Ls with 39-seat bodies, again with two doors, though LHs delivered later in the year were single-door 43-seaters.

Withdrawals from the fleets included Bristol LL and LWL single-deckers, and K, KS and KSW double-deckers.

The principal operator on the Isle of Wight, in 1970 as now, was Southern Vectis – the company name combining the Latin name for the island and reflecting the Southern Railway interest. It had been set up in a limited way in 1921 and in 1923 was reconstituted as Dodson Brothers, using the Vectis name. Southern Railway had taken over the island's railways at the time of Grouping in 1923 and in 1929 the railway acquired an interest in the business, creating the Southern Vectis Omnibus Co Ltd. When the founders retired in 1932 their interest was bought by Tilling and BAT, and on the 1941 reorganisation it passed into Tilling Group control, and therefore to the state-owned British Transport Commission like its mainland neighbour Hants & Dorset.

In 1969 Southern Vectis took over the operations of Shamrock & Rambler on the island; S&R had previously acquired the Ventnor-based Crinage and Randall businesses, and the Cowes-based Fountain Coaches and Holmes concerns.

With a heavily seasonal business, the Southern Vectis fleet had always included a number of luxury coaches to compete with other independent companies for the thriving market for local tours. Although it had received standard Bristol/ECW products, from the late 1950s it had also bought Duple-bodied Bedfords of various types, including the three-axle VAL.

Left: Hants & Dorset bought 10 Bedford VAM70 in 1968 with dual-door Willowbrook bodies. This one, seen at Swanage in 1971, has front and rear ends cut away for use on the Sandbanks ferry.
J G Carroll

Below: This Bristol RELH6G with Duple Commander IV 49-seat coachwork was added to the Hants & Dorset fleet in 1969. It is seen at Southampton railway station.
Alec Swain/Kevin Lane collection

Left: This Sandbanks view shows a former Hants & Dorset Bristol LS6G/ECW coach converted for bus duties leaving the ferry on the Swanage-Bournemouth route, followed by a Trent Leyland Leopard/Plaxton on an extended tour.
Michael Dryhurst

Below: A nearside view of one of Wilts & Dorset's Willowbrook-bodied Bedford VAM70s shows the front entrance and centre exit.
V C Jones

the company cope with the crowds who flocked to the Isle of Wight Pop Festival in August 1970, although it had to draft in buses and coaches from local operators, as well as relicensing buses that had been delicensed for withdrawal.

Southern Vectis bus routes covered the whole island with frequent services linking Ryde with Cowes, Newport with Sandown, Ryde with Bembridge, Newport with Freshwater and Ryde with Ventnor.

There were three municipal bus fleets in our South Central area in 1970, at Bournemouth, Southampton and Swindon.

The BET company played its part in Bournemouth Corporation's early services. BET wanted to run tramways in the popular seaside town and neighbouring Poole Corporation had bought the horse tram service to the Bournemouth boundary from BET. Poole leased the line to Bournemouth Corporation and the corporation negotiated with BET to control the trams within its own boundaries. This was happening in the early years of the 20th century, and soon a substantial electric tramway system stretched from Poole to Christchurch.

The bus fleet was more typically Tilling, with examples of L, LS and MW single-deckers and K, LD, FS and FLF double-deckers. With many rural routes using country lanes, small buses were necessary, and while in the 1950s Bedford OB and Dennis Ace types were used, in 1963 it had received a batch of the small underfloor-engined Bristol SUL4A with 36-seat ECW bodies.

Although it had a 1970 fleet of just under 200 vehicles, more than half of them double-deckers, Southern Vectis was probably low in the NBC priority stakes. Three Bristol VRTs that were on order were diverted to City of Oxford, but it did receive new Bristol/ECW single-deckers, 43-seat LH6Ls and 49-seat RELL6Gs, its first RELLs. It also received a new Duple Viceroy-bodied Bedford VAL70 coach. The new vehicles helped

Successful experiments with trolleybuses in 1933 led the corporation to abandon its trams by 1936 and Bournemouth boasted one of the most-admired trolleybus fleets in the country, abandoned only in 1969 when the newest trolleybuses were just seven years old.

Bournemouth also bought motorbuses, from 1906, and for many years the double-deckers shared with the trolleybuses an unusual rear entrance/front exit layout.

The 1970 Bournemouth motorbus fleet consisted of 169 vehicles, 80 per cent of them double-deckers. Leylands had been favoured for many years, though in the 1960s Daimlers had also been bought. The older Leyland Titan PD2s with full-fronted Weymann bodies were on their way out and while Weymann-

Left: Rebuilt with a bus-style destination display and painted in bus colours, a 1957 Bristol MW6G at Winchester. Although used on bus duties, it retains its coach seats and single-piece door.
Tony Wilson

Centre: Cows may safely laze. At East Boldre in July 1970, a Hants & Dorset dual-door Bristol LH6L with ECW 39-seat body, one of a number of LHs to this layout bought in 1969/70.
Martin Llewellyn

Below: Although Hants & Dorset had bought substantial numbers of Bristol L type single-deckers as well as LS and MW coaches, it only had small batches of LS and MW buses. This 1959 MW5G 43-seat bus is seen in Southampton in 1968.
Tony Wilson

Left: For the service across Poole Harbour to Swanage, Hants & Dorset owned a number of Bristol L types with special cutaway rears. New in 1950, no.663 is an LL6A and carries a 1960-built ECW 37-seat body that has traces of the bodywork built on contemporary Bristol SC4LKs. This is a view that many will recall from summer holidays in the area.
Geoff Lumb

Above: In hometown Salisbury, and looking freshly repainted in October 1971, a 1954 Wilts & Dorset Bristol LD6G with 58-seat ECW body, from the company's first Lodekka batch.
Ted Jones

Left: Sporting chrome 'dustbin-lid' style wheel centres, a smartly presented Wilts & Dorset late-model Bristol MW6G with ECW 41-seat dual-purpose body, at Salisbury depot. It was new in 1966.
Omnicolour

Left: One of the more bizarre rebuilds of a Wilts & Dorset coach for driver-only bus work – a 1958 Bristol MW6G/ECW seen leaving Salisbury in April 1970 not only in red livery with a bus destination box added, but also with a central exit door, in the fashion of the time.
Edward Shirras

Below: One of five Bedford SB13 with Duple Super Vega 41-seat coach bodies bought by Wilts & Dorset in 1965 at Victoria Coach Station, London, on Royal Blue duplicate work.
Edward Shirras

bought the assets in 1898 to prepare for electrification of the system. Electric services started in January 1900 and expanded until the 1930s when a start was made converting tram routes to motorbuses; the process was accelerated after World War 2 and the last tram ran at the end of 1949. Motorbuses had been used since 1919 and Southampton famously bought a substantial fleet of Guy Arab double-deckers in the decade after World War 2.

Since that time Southampton had bought AECs and Leylands and in the 1970 fleet were Park Royal-bodied Regent Vs and Titan PD2s dating from the early 1960s and a sizeable fleet of East Lancs-bodied Regent Vs bought between 1963 and 1967, including a number built by the East Lancs associate, Neepsend. From 1968 East Lancs-bodied Leyland Atlanteans became the standard purchase and by the early 1980s the entire normal service fleet was composed of East Lancs Atlanteans.

The small single-deck fleet in 1970 consisted of the surviving Guy Arab UFs, three Alexander-bodied Albion Nimbuses and AEC Swifts with Strachans and East Lancs bodywork.

The other municipal fleet in the area was Swindon Corporation. The town of Swindon had grown up in the 19th century around the Great Western Railway's works, and the corporation started running electric trams in 1904 and bought motorbuses from 1927 which had replaced the trams by 1929. The fleet was dominated by Daimlers for many years, though AECs and Leylands were also bought in the 1960s. In 1970 Swindon bought Northern Counties-bodied Daimler Fleetlines, its first dual-door double-deckers.

Independent bus operators in the South Central area were few and far between.

In Dorset, Bere Regis & District served rural communities in an area bounded by Bridport, Shaftesbury, Wareham and Yeovil with a fleet of 91 buses and coaches, including AECs, Bedfords and Leylands. On the Isle of Wight, Seaview Services still operated its Seaview-Ryde route.

bodied Titan PD3s had been bought between 1959 and 1963, from 1964 Bournemouth turned to rear-engined double-deckers, firstly Leyland Atlanteans and then Daimler Fleetlines including a batch of convertible open-toppers, some of which would be sold on for service in London. Two Fleetlines bought in 1964 had bodywork built in Northern Ireland by MH Cars, the only double-deckers in Britain with bodywork built there until Wright introduced its Gemini range.

Bournemouth's single-deck fleet in 1970 included older Leylands as well as Leopards bought in 1965 and examples of Daimler's ill-fated Roadliner in 1967/68.

During 1970 Bournemouth received more new Alexander-bodied Atlanteans, and in addition to Titan PD2s sold three unusual Burlingham-bodied full-fronted Leyland Tiger PS2s, which went into preservation.

City of Southampton Transport Department had 181 buses in 1970, more than 90 per cent double-deck. This great seaport had been served by horse tramways since 1879 and the corporation

The best-known of the mainland independents, King Alfred Motor Services, was still running its Winchester-based network in 1970. The business was started in 1915 by the Chisnell family, linking the city of Winchester with local army camps, but in 1921 it started running local routes within the city. From 1941 it started using double-deckers and by 1970 had built up a substantial network. The fleet in 1970 consisted of 21 double-deck and 17 single-deck buses, including such exotica as AEC Bridgemaster and Renown lowheight double-deckers, and Leyland Panther rear-engined single-deckers. There were also Roe-bodied Leyland Atlanteans.

King Alfred would remain in independent hands only until 1973 when the business was sold to Hants & Dorset, including a number of the newer buses.

That was simply a prelude to the changes that would happen following the privatisation of the National Bus Company in the 1980s. Hants & Dorset was split into several parts in 1983 as a preparation for the expected local bus deregulation. There was a belief in some parts of NBC that smaller companies would respond better in a competitive environment and so three local bus companies – Hampshire Bus, Wilts & Dorset and Provincial Bus Company – were created, along with Shamrock & Rambler Coaches and Hants & Dorset Engineering.

Hampshire Bus was a mix of the old H&D and W&D, with depots at Andover, Basingstoke, Eastleigh, Southampton and Winchester, essentially the eastern part of the combined area. The new Wilts & Dorset assumed control of the west, with depots at Blandford, Lymington, Pewsey, Poole, Ringwood, Salisbury and Swanage. Provincial's area expanded north to take in H&D's depot at Fareham bus station as well as its own Hoeford depot. Shamrock & Rambler continued the S&R coaching activities based on Bournemouth and Southampton.

Hants & Dorset Engineering was based at Eastleigh providing major engineering facilities for the four operating companies as well as handling commercial work.

In the NBC privatisation, Hampshire Bus was sold in 1987 to Skipburn Ltd, a holding company associated with Stagecoach, and the first sign of

Above: **Seen in Christchurch in 1971 on the Bournemouth-Salisbury service, a recently-delivered Wilts & Dorset Bristol RELL6G with ECW 50-seat dual-purpose body.**
W T Cansick

Left: **Wilts & Dorset received Bristol LH6Ls with unusual dual-door ECW 39-seat bodies, as shown here in Salisbury in March 1970.**
M A Penn

Above: The vehicles acquired with the Silver Star business in 1963 provided a touch of variety in the Wilts & Dorset fleet. At Salisbury depot is a 1958 Leyland Tiger Cub PSUC1/2 with 41-seat Harrington body alongside more conventional W&D fare, a 1958 Bristol MW6G coach now downgraded to bus duties.
Omnicolour

Left: A reminder of the much-missed Bournemouth trolleybus system, closed only in 1969, is provided by this 1968 view of a Wilts & Dorset 1963 Bristol Lodekka FS6B passing one of the fine Sunbeam MF2B/ Weymann trolleybuses that were destined to have only short lives in the town. No.300, seen here, was one of the last to be delivered – and one of the UK's last new trolleybuses – entering service only in 1961.
Tony Wilson

In Winchester Street, Salisbury, a Wilts & Dorset Bristol Lodekka FS6G, new in 1962 with 60-seat ECW body.
Geoff Lumb

Left: Wilts & Dorset received Bristol LH6Ls with 43-seat ECW bodies in 1970, like this example seen in Andover bus station.
Geoff Lumb

Below: Unusually for a Tilling company, Wilts & Dorset received Willowbrook-bodied Bedford VAM70 buses in 1968. One is seen at Andover bus station about to be passed by a 1955 Bristol Lodekka LD6B.
Geoff Lumb

Above: A 1959 Wilts & Dorset Bristol Lodekka LD6G lays over at Salisbury bus station.
Kevin Lane collection

Left: One of the older Bristol Lodekka LD6G in the Southern Vectis fleet. The front wings have been cut away for brake cooling, and the driver's windscreen is open, suggesting a hot day.
Edward Shirras

Stagecoach's acquisitive ambitions. It quickly sold off its Southampton area operations and these survive as Solent Blue Line, part of the Southern Vectis and subsequently Go-Ahead Group empires.

Provincial was sold later in 1987 to its management and employees on an equal co-ownership basis and would be the only NBC sale that involved all staff on this basis. As People's Provincial it continued in business until 1995 when it sold out to FirstBus.

Wilts & Dorset was sold soon afterwards to its management team and although it faced some fierce competition in its early privatised days, it survived to sell out to Go-Ahead Group in 2003.

Above: Unusual buses in the Southern Vectis fleet were the four Bristol LHS6L with Marshall 35-seat bodies.
Edward Shirras

Left: Southern Vectis received its first Bristol RELLs in 1970, two RELL6G with ECW 49-seat bodywork. More RELL6Gs arrived in 1972, but after that the company received NBC-standard Leyland Nationals.
Edward Shirras

Shamrock & Rambler went, also in 1987, to Drawlane, a predecessor of what became British Bus and eventually Arriva. It expanded into local bus work but ceased trading in 1989.

Hants & Dorset Engineering had a short life and didn't quite make it to privatisation. Part of the business, Hants & Dorset Distribution, was sold as part of a package of NBC engineering departments.

Two of the municipal fleets in the area had an interesting time. Southampton Citybus was set up as an arms-length company in 1986, to be renamed Southampton City Transport in 1993. In 1997 the municipal company passed to FirstBus.

Bournemouth Transport Ltd, the 1986 arms-length company, adopted the Yellow Buses identity and remained in local authority ownership until Transdev bought it in 2005 after a bitter battle with Go-Ahead, owners of the other major local bus operator, Wilts & Dorset.

Swindon Corporation became Thamesdown District Council in 1974 and Thamesdown Transport in 1986. It survives in 2006 as one of the dwindling band of bus companies in municipal control. ■

Above: New deliveries to Wilts & Dorset in 1970 included Bristol RELL6Gs with dual-purpose 50-seat ECW bodies.
Geoff Lumb

Right: Squeezing its way through the narrow streets of Ventnor in July 1971, a Southern Vectis 1959 Bristol Lodekka LD6G with ECW 60-seat body, one of more than 60 bought between 1954 and 1959.
Tony Wilson

Below: Ticket to Ryde? An early-style Southern Vectis Bristol LD6G, new in 1956, sits on Ryde Esplanade.
Tony Wilson

Above: For more rural services, Southern Vectis bought a batch of eight Bristol SUL4A with 36-seat ECW bodies. One is seen at Luccombe in 1971.
Tony Wilson

Below: Southern Vectis operated many Bedfords over the years on coach touring duties on the Isle of Wight. This 1966 VAL14 with 52-seat Duple Vega Major body is seen at Sandown in 1976.
Tony Wilson

Above: Withdrawal of Hants & Dorset's famous fleet of open-top Bristol Ks started in 1970 but FRU 304 had found its way across the Solent to Southern Vectis in 1965 with two others, where it is seen in Ventnor in 1971. A 1944 K5G, it carries a rebuilt 1938 Brush 59-seat body.
Tony Wilson

Above: **Southern Vectis converted its older Bristol LS6G coaches for bus duties later in their life. This 1952 example with the original style of ECW windscreen, has received a destination display and an inward-opening folding door.**
Edward Shirras

Below: **A 1969 Bedford VAM70 with Duple Viceroy 45-seat body in the Southern Vectis coaching fleet.**
Edward Shirras

Above: A late-model Bristol MW6G with 45-seat ECW body for the Southern Vectis fleet. It was new in 1966.
Edward Shirras

Right: After many years when it bought dual-door double-deckers, Bournemouth Corporation went for more conventional forward entrance vehicles for its 1963 delivery of Weymann-bodied Leyland Titan PD3A/1s.
Peter J Walnes

Above: Photographed at Westbourne in 1966, a 1965 Bournemouth Corporation Daimler Fleetline CRG6LX with Weymann 74-seat bodywork. It has the pseudo-Alexander style of front end applied to several Weymann-bodied double-deckers at this time.
Tony Wilson

Left: Weymann bodywork on a Bournemouth Leyland Atlantean PDR1/1, seen in the town centre along with a Weymann-bodied Leyland Titan PD3. Note the overhead wiring still in place at the end of trolleybus operation in 1969.
Geoff Lumb

Right: Unique vehicles for a British mainland fleet were the two Daimler Fleetline CRG6LX with MH Cars bodywork, built in Northern Ireland for Bournemouth Corporation in 1964.
Geoff Lumb

Left: After the Bournemouth trolleybuses were withdrawn, vehicles continued to use the famous turntable at Christchurch. The driver and conductor are using muscle-power to turn this 1960 Leyland Titan PD3/1 with Weymann bodywork. The turntable still exists, with a commemorative plaque on a nearby building.
Geoff Lumb

Below: Bournemouth bought 11 Daimler Roadliners with Willowbrook 49-seat bodies in 1967/68, though reputedly no more than five of the nine were ever in service at the same time. This one is seen in February 1970.
Martin Llewellyn/Omnicolour

Above: In addition to the 10 closed-top Weymann-bodied Daimler
Fleetlines received by Bournemouth Corporation in 1965, there
were 10 of these open-top versions, each named after an English
county; this is *Yorkshire*. Seven of the open-toppers were bought
by London Transport in 1977, though not the bus in the photo at
Tuckton Bridge.
Michael Dryhurst

Below: In 1965 Bournemouth Corporation bought three of these
Leyland Leopard PSU3/2R with Weymann 45-seat dual-purpose
bodies, complete with roof quarterlights. One is seen at the Pier.
B A Jenkins

Left: A fine official view of a 1967 Swindon Corporation Daimler CVG6.30 with Northern Counties 70-seat forward-entrance body, one of three bought that year that proved to be the undertaking's last front-engined double-deckers.

Below: Another manufacturer's view, showing one of five Swindon AEC Reliances with Willowbrook 41-seat dual-door bodies bought in 1964; another six were bought the following year.

Right: Southampton Corporation famously bought a massive fleet of nearly 200 Park Royal-bodied Guy Arab III double-deckers in the decade after World War 2, like this well turned-out 1949 example.
Geoff Lumb

Below: In the 1960s Southampton had bought Leyland Titans and AEC Regent Vs. An attractive Neepsend-bodied Regent V sits ahead of a rather less attractive Park Royal-bodied Titan PD2A/27.
Royston Morgan

Southampton then went on to build up a substantial fleet of East Lancs-bodied Leyland Atlanteans; this was a 1969 PDR1A/1.
Geoff Lumb

The later livery style helped to slightly improve the looks of the Southampton Park Royal-bodied Leyland Titan PD2A/27s bought in 1962/63.
Geoff Lumb

Swindon Corporation received its first dual-door Daimler Fleetlines in 1970, CRG6LX models with 71-seat Northern Counties bodies.
Geoff Lumb

Above: A Swindon scene with a corporation Daimler CVG6/
Park Royal, new in 1957, about to be passed by a Bristol Omnibus
Company Lodekka.
Kevin Lane collection

Below: An unusual bus in the Southampton Corporation fleet,
a 1957 Albion Nimbus MR9N with Alexander 31-seat body,
at Swaythling in 1968.
G J Wadley

Above: Park Royal used Bridgemaster parts to build this rather
ungainly bodywork for Southampton Corporation on Leyland
Titan PD2/27 chassis in 1960/61.
Michael Dryhurst

Below: Southampton bought AEC Swifts in the late 1960s. This is
one of four MP2R models bought in 1967/68 with 47-seat dual-door
bodywork built by Strachans at nearby Hamble. The body style is
similar to that on London Transport's prototype AEC Merlins.
M A Penn

Above: An older Swindon Northern Counties Fleetline in the town centre in July 1970.

Martin Llewellyn

Right: Swindon standardised on Daimlers for many years, most with Park Royal bodies. Among the more unusual ones were three 1953 Freelines with standee-type centre-entrance 34-seat bodies; one is seen in Manchester Street, Swindon, in October 1969.

Ted Jones

Above: Another view of a Southampton Strachans-bodied AEC Swift, in the 1970s in Bournemouth bus station on hire to Hants & Dorset.

J G Carroll

Below: Southampton's four 1969 Swift 2MP2Rs had East Lancs 47-seat bodywork, as seen in the city centre in October 1970.

M A Penn

King Alfred bus services started from Winchester Broadway in the shadow of the statue of King Alfred. Passing the statue is one of the two Willowbrook-bodied Leyland Leopards.
Michael Dryhurst

After buying various Leyland and AEC front-engined models, King Alfred turned to the rear-engined Leyland Atlantean in 1967 when it bought four PDR1/2 models with 74-seat Roe bodywork.
Michael Dryhurst

Above: Leyland contrast at Winchester Broadway. The Plaxton-bodied Panther PSUR1A/1, one of three new in 1970 to the local independent, King Alfred, passes one of the buses they would replace, a 1950 all-Leyland Titan PD2/1. The Panther passed into the Hants & Dorset fleet following the 1973 acquisition of the King Alfred business.
Chris Aston/Omnicolour

Left: An older King Alfred Leyland, a 1962 Leopard PSU3/2R with 51-seat Willowbrook body, at Winchester Broadway. This bus also passed to Hants & Dorset.
Geoff Lumb

Left: A well-known bus in the King Alfred fleet was this Park Royal-bodied AEC Regent V. Built in 1956 as an AEC demonstrator, it passed to King Alfred in 1958.
Geoff Lumb

West of England

Those old Ian Allan British Bus Fleet ABCs called it 'West of England', that beautiful area west of Somerset and Dorset that takes in Devon and Cornwall. For hundreds of thousands of visitors each year it was – and is – a popular tourist draw, offering everything from the beautiful beaches in areas like Torbay, North Devon, Newquay and St Ives, to the dramatic Bodmin Moor and Dartmoor and the rugged Cornwall coast. It was never easy operating territory for bus operators, combining deeply rural services with seasonal services aimed at tourists.

Some of the earliest motorbus services in Britain ran in the West Country as the Great Western Railway company introduced bus services in the early years of the 20th century to provide links with its trains. For a period the GWR Road Motor

Department had the biggest bus fleet in the country and although London quickly overtook it once it had got its act together, it still had 115 vehicles when its buses passed into the newly-formed Western National company in 1929. Western National and Southern National were owned jointly by the National Omnibus & Transport company and the Great Western and Southern railways. National had been operating in the area since 1919 and had grown by acquisition in the 1920s; it was taken over by Tilling in 1931 and continued to grow in a series of takeovers during the 1930s.

The names of the two companies and their operating areas reflected the railway company involvement. Southern National's operating area was in two distinct parts. One was in the western

Above: Bristol K types were the mainstay of many Southern National and Western National services from the 1940s through to the 1960s and some survived into the 1970s. Turning off the Esplanade at Weymouth in July 1969 is a 1953 KSW6B with 55-seat lowbridge ECW bodywork, a late survivor of the large fleet of LTA-registered buses bought by the company between 1950 and 1953.
Martin Llewellyn

Left: Another late-surviving Western National Bristol K type, a 1950 KS5G with lowbridge ECW 55-seat body, at Dartmouth in 1969.
Royston Morgan

part of Dorset and had boundaries with Hants & Dorset to the east, Western National to the north and west, and Devon General on its south-east edge. The other swept from the North Devon coast at Lynmouth, south to Newquay. Separating the two parts of Southern National were Western National and the BET Group's Devon General company. Western National too was divided, its northern area in Somerset and Wiltshire, its south-western part covering much of Cornwall as well as part of Devon.

Southern National's main depots were at Barnstaple, Bideford, Bridport, Bude, Ilfracombe, Seaton, Weymouth and Yeovil. Western National's main depots were at Bridgewater, Callington, Camborne, Falmouth, Helston, Minehead, Newquay, Penzance, Plymouth, St Austell, Taunton, Tavistock, Totnes, Trowbridge and Truro.

Although they covered an apparently large and complex area, Southern and Western National effectively operated as one company, albeit with different fleetnames. Under NBC the situation had been formalised with the dropping of the Southern National fleetname from November 1969. Western National's large fleet – 935 buses in 1970 – placed it among the 10 largest NBC fleets at the time.

Many of Southern National's most frequent services were based on Weymouth, long trunk routes running inland to Salisbury and west to Exeter. Western National operated frequent services from Plymouth to Torquay and less frequent services to Exeter, Bideford and Bude. In North Devon its services included links along the coast between Ilfracombe, Lynmouth and Minehead.

There was a third major element to Western National, the famous coaching company Royal Blue. Back in 1880 Thomas Elliott had started a horse-drawn coach linking Bournemouth, which had no railway station at the time, with Holmsley Station on the main London & South Western Railway main line. Elliott Brothers (Bournemouth) Ltd, using the fleetname Royal Blue, moved to motor vehicles from 1911 and in the 1920s started first long-distance motorcoach services between Bournemouth and

London. In 1935 Royal Blue was bought by Southern and Western National, and although the private hire, excursion and tour side passed to Hants & Dorset, the long-distance coaching business stayed with the two National companies and developed greatly in the 1930s and 1950s. Coaches represented a quarter of the 1970 Western National fleet, and although not all were liveried for Royal Blue operations, it indicates the continued importance of the express network.

Royal Blue's extensive network covered the main routes linking London with the major centres in Hampshire, Wiltshire, Devon and Cornwall, and by 1970, as a result of its involvement with other NBC companies in the Associated Motorways coach service network, centred on Cheltenham, and joint services with other operators, Royal Blue coaches also operated along the south coast to Sussex and Kent,

Above: Bristol LS type single-deckers were bought by Western/Southern National between 1952 and 1957. At Yeovil in March 1970 sit two LS5G buses with 45-seat ECW bodies, one displaying the then-obsolete Southern National fleetname and the other the newer, simplified Western National name.
M A Penn

Left: When photographed in January 1971, this was the only Bristol KSW type still in regular passenger service at Western National's Weymouth depot, and is seen in Bournemouth working a special for the Dorset Transport Circle.
C L Caddy

north to Birmingham, Bristol, Cheltenham, Gloucester and Oxford, and even into East Anglia.

All but a handful of the buses in the combined fleet of 935 buses and coaches were standard Tilling-issue Bristols with ECW bodies. There were Bristol L, LS, MW, SU, RE and LH type single-deckers, and K, FS, FSF, FLF and VRT double-deckers. The only non-Bristols in the fleet were Bedfords, VAM5 types bought in 1967 and fitted with ECW 41-seat bus bodies. These were a stopgap between the Bristol SU type, of which Western/Southern National was the largest user, and the LH.

Delivered to Western National in 1970 were more new single-deck buses, LH6Ls and RELL6Gs, and RELH6G coaches. Unusual additions for the Royal Blue fleet were 12 Bristol LH6Ls with Duple Commander IV bodies; previously Royal Blue coaches had been built on heavyweight chassis. On the way out were L and LS buses, the last of the Royal Blue LS6G coaches, and KS and KSW double-deckers.

Another 1970 development provided a foretaste of later and more major changes to NBC's express coach operation. The Royal Blue coaches and those of two other local NBC coach fleets, Greenslades and Grey Cars, were painted in broken white with broad coloured waistbands – blue for Royal Blue, green for Greenslades and grey for Grey Cars. Other NBC fleets would adopt liveries based on the same scheme, but these would all disappear with the introduction of National Express white.

The former BET Group 'interloper' in the south-west, surrounded on all sides by Tilling influence, was the splendidly-named Devon General Omnibus & Touring company. Devon General served the Torbay resorts from Brixham to Seaton with an inland network of rural routes. Its territory was bounded by Honiton, Okehampton and

Tiverton, with routes radiating out from Exeter.

It was in Exeter that the company started up, in 1919, but competition with the National Electric Construction Company's Torquay Tramways company led to the tramway company buying and re-forming Devon General. The two local railway companies, the Great Western and the Southern, jointly bought a half stake in Devon General in 1929 and the railway investment promoted acquisition and expansion. In 1931 NEC was bought by BET.

Among the Devon General acquisitions was Grey Cars of Torquay and although the company was wound up the Grey Cars name and livery was retained for DG's coaching fleet.

Devon General had reached agreements with its neighbouring operators, Southern and Western National, over the transfer of routes wholly within DG territory and joint operation of longer-distance routes that crossed boundaries. This happened in 1938

Above: **After the Bristol LS, Western/Southern National bought the Bristol MW with both bus and coach bodies. This is an early-model MW5G with 45-seat ECW body, new in 1958 and seen at Exeter.**
W T Cansick

Right: **A rear view of a 1959 Western National Bristol Lodekka LD6B at Paignton bus station.**
W T Cansick

Above: From 1953 until 1966 Western/Southern National bought various versions of the Bristol/ECW Lodekka. At St Ives in June 1970 are a 1955 LD6B, on the right, and a 1965 FLF6B.
Royston Morgan

Left: Western National was an early customer for Bristol's VRT model, taking 10 in 1969. In Plymouth, on Exeter Street with Breton Side bus station visible below, a VRT heads for Saltash. In the bus station are other Western National buses, as well as a Royal Blue coach and Plymouth Corporation vehicles.
Geoff Lumb

Below: Seasonal services in Cornwall and North Devon kept Western/Southern National busy. At St Ives in June 1970 is a selection of Western National vehicles – two Lodekkas on the right, a 1958 LD6G and a cream-painted 1964 FLF6G, and a 1970 Royal Blue Bristol LH6L with 41-seat Duple Commander coach body, wearing the newly introduced 'south-west' coach livery.
Royston Morgan

Western/Southern National built up the largest fleet of Bristol's Albion-engined SU model, taking 133 between 1960 and 1966. They were delivered in short SUS and longer SUL versions, and as buses and coaches. Caught in Plymouth is a 1961 SUL4A with 36-seat ECW bus body, left, alongside a rare Bedford VAM5 with 41-seat ECW body, one of 12 bought in 1967 to bridge the one-year gap between the Bristol SU and LH models.
Geoff Lumb

In the early 1970s two rare Western National Bristol Lodekka LDL6Gs were converted to open-top layout, as seen here at Falmouth. The LDL was the 30ft-long version of the LD, with 70 seats. It carries the name *Admiral Boscawen*.
Royston Morgan

Loading at St Ives in July 1969 for the service to Penzance, a 1955 Bristol LD6B, complete with platform doors, illustrates the pre-NBC Western National livery well, complete with its fleetnumber plates.
Martin Llewellyn/Omnicolour

and in 1947 agreement was reached with Exeter City Transport leading to the creation of Exeter Joint Services, which resulted in DG buses operating wholly within Exeter and city buses operating well out into the surrounding area; mileages and receipts were pooled.

Devon General's bus fleet provided variety in an area dominated by Bristol/ECW products. AEC chassis were favoured for many years and the 1970 fleet of 275 buses and coaches included 194 AECs, 72 Leylands and nine Albions. The AECs were Reliance single-deckers and Regent V double-deckers, and the Leylands were Atlanteans, including convertible open-toppers for use in the Torbay area. The Albions were midi-size Nimbuses for rural routes.

The formation of National Bus Company was to have a dramatic impact on Devon General. For a start the company's head office moved from Torquay to Exeter and the responsibility for Grey Cars tours from Exeter passed to Greenslades, another NBC company. More significant was the decision of Exeter Corporation to sell its transport undertaking to NBC early in 1970, and control was passed to Devon General. Even more significant was the transfer of the Devon General company into Western National control on 1 January 1971, although the Devon General name survived for a while.

Greenslades Tours Ltd has been mentioned in this chapter. It started near Exeter in 1912, grew in the 1920s and 1930s and branched into extended tour work in 1948. The company was bought by BET in 1953 and continued to buy up other local touring companies. Its 1970 fleet of 75 coaches consisted of AEC Reliances with bodies by Duple, Harrington and Plaxton. Greenslades would pass to National Travel in 1973.

Exeter City Transport started 1970 in municipal control, but as we have seen in April it was sold to NBC and control passed to Devon General.

In 1903 Exeter Corporation bought the Exeter Tramways Company which had operated horse trams since 1882, relaid the track and electrified and extended the system. The corporation bought its first motorbuses in 1929 and by 1931 the tramway system had been replaced by buses. The 1970 Exeter City Transport fleet of 65 buses comprised 45 Leylands and 20 Guys, with bodywork by a number of builders, including 40 by Massey. Sixty-five buses were transferred into the DG fleet – the oldest being all-Leyland Titan PD2/1s dating from 1948 and the rest were a mix of newer Leyland PD2s and Guy Arabs plus the undertaking's newest purchases, Massey-bodied two-door Leyland Leopard and Panther single-deckers. Marshall-bodied Panthers that had been ordered by Exeter were delivered to Devon General/Western National in 1970/71.

The one other municipality in the south-west was Plymouth City Transport. Company horse (and briefly steam) trams provided the first street transport in the area, but Plymouth Corporation bought the horse tram operation in 1892, introduced electric trams in 1899 and motorbuses

Above: A well-loaded 1962 Western National Bristol Lodekka FLF6B/ECW in Paignton.
W T Cansick

Left: Among Western/Southern National's large fleet of Bristol SUs were ECW coach-bodied models, like this 1962 SUL4A 33-seater, at Victoria Coach Station, London in 1969 at the start of what could have been a noisy journey to Dartmouth on Royal Blue duty.
W T Cansick

from 1929. Most of the trams were replaced by buses in the 1930s but one route survived to 1945. Plymouth was badly bombed during World War 2 and because the bus operators suffered badly at this time the corporation and Western National entered a pooling agreement in 1942 where mileage and profits on Plymouth Joint Services was apportioned on an 80:20 basis to the corporation and the company. This situation would survive for a number of years.

In 1970 Plymouth had an all double-deck fleet of 233 buses, all Leylands with four in every five bodies built by Metro-Cammell. During the year it introduced long-wheelbase 33ft Leyland Atlanteans with dual-door Park Royal bodies for driver-only double-deck services, which had been introduced in September 1969. Out of the fleet went the last of many Leyland-bodied Leyland Titans that had been bought over the years.

Many of the smaller independent bus service operators in the south-west had been snapped up by the big area agreement companies, but one notable survivor was Hutchings & Cornelius Services of South Petherton, Somerset. Its origins were in two separate companies operating bus services around Yeovil, Taunton and Ilminster, which linked in 1934. In 1970 H&C made a number of changes, including concentrating its fleet in South Petherton. H&C famously bought a new Dennis Loline, and would later buy a new Bristol VRT, both unusual purchases for an independent operator. Its main routes linked South Petherton with Taunton and Yeovil. H&C's 1970 fleet of 19 buses and coaches included nine Dennises and five AECs.

Top: After the Bristol SU and a brief flirtation with Bedford VAM5s, Western/Southern National turned to Bristol's LH model. This 1970 LH6L with 43-seat ECW body is at Woolacombe.
Kevin Lane collection

Centre: Another Bristol LH6L, a Southern National version at Yeovil bus station in 1968.
Michael Bennett

Left: Leaving Bournemouth bound for Weymouth, a Southern National Bristol RELL6G with shallow-screen flat-front ECW 53-seat body.
B W Spencer

Above: The shape of things to come at Western National, a 1971 Leyland Atlantean PDR1/3 with Alexander 73-seat body, one of five transferred to Western National in 1972 and photographed in pre-NBC livery with simplified fleetnames.

Royston Morgan

Below: At Paignton bus station, a Royal Blue Bristol MW6G with 39-seat ECW coach body from the Western National fleet.

Tony Wilson

Above: Later Bristol MW coaches for the Royal Blue carried the revised style of ECW coachwork, as seen at St Ives in June 1970.
Royston Morgan

Below: From 1964, new coaches for the Royal Blue fleet were RELH6Gs with 45-seat ECW bodies, though this 1968 example carries Western National fleetnames.
Royston Morgan

Also based in South Petherton was the Gunn family's Safeway Services, also operating into Yeovil and serving many smaller villages. The 1970 Safeway fleet of 10 vehicles was made up of three buses and seven coaches, mainly Bedfords. In 1979 the Hutchings & Cornelius business closed down and Safeway took over the South Petherton/Crewkerne-Yeovil services as well as three buses.

As a preparation for deregulation, in 1983 Western National was split into four smaller companies. Western National's area was redefined to cover Plymouth and west to Cornwall, based in Plymouth; the Southern National name was resurrected to cover Somerset and Dorset, based in Weymouth; Devon General was resurrected to cover much of its old area in Exeter and Torbay, based in Torquay; and a new name, North Devon, covered the area suggested by its name, based in Barnstaple.

Devon General was famously the first bus company to be sold in the NBC sell-off, to its management team led by Harry Blundred, while Western National followed a year later, initially to Plympton Coachlines, with a stake held by Badgerline; Southern National and North Devon were among the last NBC sales, in a joint purchase by Southern National's management team.

After a few buccaneering years, Devon General found itself as

part of the Stagecoach empire, while Southern National, owned by Cawlett Ltd, acquired several other local companies to strengthen its operations, but sold out to FirstGroup in 1999; Western National passed to Badgerline and then into FirstGroup, where it eventually ended up back in the same ownership as Southern National and North Devon, effectively reconstituting the old Western National company.

Plymouth City Transport became Plymouth Citybus in 1986 and survives in local authority ownership. ∎

Left: Western/Southern National bought 68 Bristol RELL6G between 1967 and 1973. This is a 1971 example in Barnstaple when new.
Edward Shirras

Below left: An early Western National Bristol Lodekka, a 1954 LD6B, sits at Dartmouth station in 1969.
Kevin Lane collection

Right: Carrying Western National, Devon General and Greenslades names, this 1952 Bristol LS5G was in use as a Mobile Training Unit at the Devon General garage at Torquay in 1973.
W T Cansick

Below: On driver training duties in Torquay in 1973, a Western National 1954 Bristol LD6B.
N Callow

In 1964 Devon General bought four AEC Reliance 2MU3RA with 7ft 6in-wide Harrington bodies for its Grey Cars coaching fleet. Like other local coach operators it needed coaches narrower than the standard 8ft width to negotiate roads and bridges in the Dartmoor area. This has a Cavalier body with Grenadier-style front, and shows the traditional Grey Cars livery off to good effect.
Royston Morgan

An older Grey Cars AEC Reliance, a 2MU3RV model bought in 1961 with Willowbrook Viscount bodywork, is seen at Exeter bus station.
Geoff Lumb

Under the south-west livery scheme, Grey Cars vehicles received what the photographer describes on the slide mount as the 'new horrible livery', not perhaps the most successful application of this style. It is carried by a former Black & White Daimler Roadliner SRP8 with Plaxton body. Black & White had been the best coach customer for Daimler's ill-fated Roadliner, buying 37 between 1966 and 1970.
Royston Morgan

Seen in 1970, a 1963 AEC Reliance 2MU4RA with 36-seat Harrington bodywork in the Greenslades Tours fleet.
Martin Llewellyn/Omnicolour

For years AECs had dominated the Devon General fleet. Among the last double-deck AECs bought were Willowbrook-bodied 59-seaters like this Regent V seen in Torquay in June 1970.
Royston Morgan

In a sea of red and cream at Newton Abbot bus station in 1970, a 1959 Devon General AEC Reliance 2MU3RV with 41-seat Willowbrook bus body.
Royston Morgan

Above: Climbing westbound out of Lyme Regis bound for
Exmouth in April 1969, a 1960 Royal Blue Bristol MW6G with
39-seat ECW coach body.
Edward Shirras

Below: Two 1969 Royal Blue Bristol RELH6G/ECW coaches parked
up at London's Victoria Coach Station, ready for their return
journeys to the south-west.
Kevin Lane collection

Above: Western National continued to buy Bristol RELH6G for the Royal Blue fleet until 1974, the later deliveries carrying Plaxton Panorama Elite bodies like this one seen in Paignton in 1971.
M A Penn

Below: Wearing the Greenslades version of the south-west coach livery, a 1969 AEC Reliance/Duple Commander IV at Torquay in 1971.
Alec Swain/Kevin Lane collection

Left: For its lightly-loaded routes Devon General used Albion Nimbuses, including three 1962 examples with attractive Harrington 31-seat bodies.
Geoff Lumb

Centre: A Devon General AEC Reliance 2MU3RV, one of seven bought in 1963 with 41-seat BET-style Marshall bodies.
Royston Morgan

Below: A later Devon General AEC Reliance, a 1967 2MU3RA with 39-seat BET-style Marshall body, at Bampton in 1970.
Chris Aston

In 1961 Devon General famously bought a batch of nine convertible open-top Leyland Atlantean PDR1/1 with Metro-Cammell 75-seat bodies for services in Torbay. The 'Sea Dog' class all carried names; this is *Earl Howe*.
Chris Aston/Omnicolour

Wearing the final style of Devon General livery, without the cream band under the upper deck windows, a 1960 Leyland Atlantean PDR1/1 with Roe 75-seat body, in Torquay in 1971.
Royston Morgan

Following the acquisition of the Exeter City Transport business in 1970, the buses involved had 200 added to their fleetnumbers. In Exeter bus station, now numbered 251, is a 1956 Guy Arab IV with Massey 56-seat body. Some of these buses would last with Western National well into the 1970s.
Geoff Lumb

Above: **Two AEC Reliances at Dartmouth early in 1970, a Grey Cars example with Duple Commander body and a Greenslades coach with Harrington Cavalier body.**

Royston Morgan

Below: **Devon General's engineering department van stands by in this June 1969 scene – perhaps to repair the collapsed destination blind on this 1965 AEC Regent V/Park Royal forward entrance 69-seater.**

Kevin Lane collection

Above: A 1959 Devon General Leyland Atlantean/Metro-Cammell awaits its crew at Teignmouth in January 1970. Behind is a Park Royal-bodied AEC Regent V.
Royston Morgan

Below: Wearing a reversed style of livery in 1971 at Exeter bus station, a 1968 Devon General AEC Reliance 6U3ZR with 47-seat Willowbrook body.
Edward Shirras

Above: Plymouth City Transport was a staunch Leyland fan, and in 1970 the fleet included Titans and Atlanteans. This is a 1957 Titan PD2/40 with Metro-Cammell 56-seat body, one of 90 bought between 1955 and 1958.
Martin Llewellyn/ Omnicolour

Left: Plymouth bought its first Atlanteans in 1960; this is a 1963 PDR1/1 with Metro-Cammell 77-seat body. Note the large shaded tramway-style fleetnumbers.
Geoff Lumb

Top: A busy 1970 scene on Royal Parade, Plymouth, with a corporation Titan PD2/40 with Metro-Cammell bodywork and three Leyland Atlanteans, most prominently a 1964 PDR1/1, again with Metro-Cammell body.
Martin Llewellyn

Above: From 1968 Plymouth bought the 33ft-long PDR2/1 Atlantean. This is a 1969 example with dual-door 77-seat Park Royal bodywork.
Omnicolour

Right: Hutchings & Cornelius was one of the best-known independent fleets in the south-west, buying a high proportion of new buses, like this 1969 AEC Reliance 6MU3R with Willowbrook 45-seat body.
Geoff Lumb

Above: With the 1969 delivery of AEC Reliance 6MU3R/Marshall 39-seaters Devon General adopted a simpler livery style, with all-cream roof.
Edward Shirras

Below: Although it had been principally a double-deck fleet for some years, latterly the Exeter municipal fleet also included single-deckers; this is a 1966 Leyland Leopard PSU4/2R with 41-seat Massey dual-door body, seen in 1969.
Kevin Lane collection

Above: Many of the Exeter City Transport Leylands lasted well into the 1970s with Devon General. This 1961 Titan PD2A/30 with Massey 57-seat body is seen in Devon General's traditional livery but with NBC-style fleetnames.

Royston Morgan

Below: Plymouth City Transport's first batch of 33ft-long Leyland Atlanteans arrived in 1968, PDR2/1 models with 77-seat dual-door Park Royal bodies.

R Johnson

Above: An interesting selection at Yeovil bus station in 1969, with two Hutchings & Cornelius buses, an AEC Reliance 6MU3R/ Willowbrook 45-seater and the famous East Lancs-bodied Dennis Loline, as well as a Safeway Bedford SB/Duple bus.
Martin Llewellyn

Below: Squeezing through a seemingly impossible gap in the village of Mousehole, a former Halifax Albion Nimbus/Weymann on the local service operated by Harvey of Mousehole. This bus represented the operator's entire fleet at the time.
Chris Aston

Bristol and Gloucestershire

The British Bus Fleets descriptions don't work quite so well with the remaining part of the area covered by this book. Recognising the importance of the Bristol Omnibus Co Ltd, Ian Allan had produced separate ABCs for this operator right back to 1949 when it was still the Bristol Tramways & Carriage Co Ltd, a title that reflected the company's 19th century origins.

The Bristol Tramways company had started a horse tram service in 1875, tried horse buses in 1877 and in 1886 created the Bristol Cab Company, which built up a large fleet of horse-drawn carriages of all types. The Bristol Tramways & Carriage company brought the tramway and cab companies together. BTCC was an electric tramway pioneer, opening its first route in 1895, and in 1906 tried motorbuses on the Clifton route. This was the start of what grew to be a considerable motorbus empire and the company built up a network of services into the country areas beyond the city of Bristol.

Bristol started to build its own motorbus bodies in 1907, then its own chassis from 1909, by which time it was setting up branches at Bath, Cheltenham, Gloucester and Weston-super-Mare. Like many other successful companies it grew by acquisition, including the pioneering long-distance coaching concern, Greyhound Motors of Bristol.

The Great Western Railway company bought a controlling interest in BTCC in 1929 and in 1931 control was passed to Western National. In 1936 BTCC bought Bath Electric Tramways and Bath Tramways Motor Company and the same year Gloucester City bus services were leased from the corporation. Bristol buses replaced the trams in Weston-super-Mare in 1937 and Bath in 1939, and in 1937 had reached

agreement with Bristol Corporation to create Bristol Joint Services; under this arrangement BTCC became the manager and, with the corporation, a joint owner of the city transport system. Bristol's last trams operated in 1941, the closure being accelerated by serious enemy action.

When, as a Tilling company, BTCC passed to the British Transport Commission there were boundary reorganisations that resulted in Bristol gaining the Stroud area operations of Red & White and Western National, and losing its Forest of Dean services to Red & White. The acquisition of the Red & White group by BTC also brought its Cheltenham District subsidiary into Bristol control.

Bristol chassis had become the standard for the Tilling Group under BTC and were available to the Scottish Bus Group and London Transport. In addition Bristol built truck chassis for British Road Services, again part of BTC. In 1955 the chassis manufacturing business was hived off into a separate organisation, Bristol Commercial Vehicles Ltd, and in 1957 the Bristol Tramways & Carriage Co was renamed simply Bristol Omnibus Co Ltd.

As the company had grown massively from its original Bristol base, even this name was a bit of a misnomer, but with Bristol as the regional capital it reflected the economy of the area.

In spite of its name the tentacles of the Bristol Omnibus Company reached out well beyond that city. This delightful June 1970 view is in Burford, Oxfordshire, and shows a 1965 BOC Bristol MW5G with ECW 45-seat body about to return to Cheltenham.
Tony Wilson

The Bristol Omnibus territory had boundaries with a host of companies now together under the NBC umbrella. In the north there was the former BET Group Midland Red empire, and proceeding clockwise was City of Oxford (BET), Thames Valley (Tilling), Wilts & Dorset (Tilling), Western National (Tilling) and Red & White (Tilling). The company's routes stretched from Great Malvern in the north to Oxford in the east, Salisbury in the south and, following the opening of the original Severn Bridge in 1966, to Cardiff in the west.

In 1970 most of the company's buses wore a green/cream livery, but the Cheltenham District fleet was painted red/cream, and the coach fleet was in cream/dark red with the Bristol Greyhound name; the name had been revived in 1952 but in 1960 the livery had been changed from cream/green. During 1970 Bristol adopted the coaching colour scheme introduced on other vehicles in NBC's south-west area, basically white but with a broad magenta waistband and prominent fleetname.

For years the Bristol company's buses had worn the Bristol city coat-of-arms as a fleetname, but increasingly a plain BRISTOL name had been introduced, and then a fleetname based on the 'Bristol' scroll; on Bristol city buses a small coat-of-arms sat atop the scroll. Buses on Gloucester City services carried a suitable fleetname and coat-of-arms, and although Bristol's two Bath subsidiaries were absorbed in 1969 the Bath names would survive on local buses for a number of years.

In addition to the urban networks in Bristol, Bath, Cheltenham and Gloucester, Bristol Omnibus operated local services in Weston-super-Mare and a vast range of country services.

The fleet in 1970 totalled 1,228 buses and coaches, plus a further 34 in the Cheltenham District fleet. Apart from one vehicle it was 100 per cent of Bristol/ECW manufacture, as you might expect, with examples of virtually every model variant that had been built, including several prototypes. As the parent company of the

Top: Bristol Omnibus operated Bristol KSW types long after many other former Tilling Group fleets had withdrawn them, mainly because BOC was a late customer for the model. This 1956 KSW6G with 60-seat ECW normal height body is seen in Bath in 1971.
Michael Dryhurst

Centre: The Cheltenham District fleet also used Bristol KSW types; this 1956 example is seen in the maroon and cream livery.
Edward Shirras

Left: The driver takes a chance to catch up on some reading at Cheltenham between journeys; his steed is a 1958 Lodekka.
Edward Shirras

now-separate Bristol Commercial Vehicles company, it was well used to proving new types on their home ground; vehicles from the Bristol fleet were also used as 'demonstrators' to other Tilling and Scottish group fleets.

Double-deckers accounted for nearly 60 per cent of the 1970 fleet but new deliveries that year were all single-deckers. There were RELL6L dual-door 44-seat buses, including examples for the Bath and Cheltenham fleets (including the company's 200th RE), RELH6L dual-purpose 49-seaters, and examples of the shorter RESL6L model. The one non-Bristol in the fleet, a Trojan that was used on a service to the Pump Room in Bath, was replaced by another non-Bristol, a Ford Transit with Strachans 16-seat body.

Withdrawals in 1970 included Bristol KSWs and LDs, and

transfers to other fleets included SUS4As to Thames Valley and 27 FLF6Gs to NBC's recently-acquired West Riding subsidiary, which was saddled with a fleet of unreliable Guy Wulfrunian double-deckers. The FLFs came from the Bristol City fleet and caused some older KSWs to be relicensed until new single-deckers came on stream.

Acquired by Bristol Omnibus in 1970 were the two prototype Bristol VRX double-deckers; these had been owned by Bristol Commercial Vehicles and painted in Bristol Omnibus and Central SMT colours for use as demonstrators, but with the decision to opt for the VRT with transverse engine rather than the longitudinally-mounted engine of the VRX prototypes, they required to find a permanent home.

At the start of 1970 Bristol Omnibus took over the Trowbridge

and Chippenham area services of Western National, together with Trowbridge depot and 24 buses. These were Bristol/ECW products – LS6Gs, LS5Gs, KSW6Bs, FSF6Gs and FLF6Bs; the FSFs had originally been Bristol Omnibus vehicles.

At the end of 1970 two Leyland Leopards with Plaxton Panorama Elite coach bodies were received for the Bristol Greyhound fleet and this marked the start of a move away from the dominant Bristol/ECW combination, particularly when Leyland National deliveries started in 1972 following the withdrawal of the RE chassis from the home market lists.

The Bristol city and country networks were split in the 1980s when several new companies were created. Bristol Omnibus, using the City Line name, was left with the Greater Bristol network; Badgerline Ltd, based at Weston-super-Mare, took over the country services based at the depots at Bristol, Bath, Wells and Weston; Cheltenham & Gloucester took over the northern part of the area, with depots at Cheltenham, Gloucester, Stroud and Swindon.

In the NBC privatisation, Badgerline was one of the first sales, and in September 1986 went to a team led by Trevor Smallwood. Bristol Omnibus went a year later to Midland Red West in partnership with the Bristol management. Cheltenham & Gloucester was another early sale and it went to its management team under the name Western Travel. Badgerline went on to buy a number of former NBC

Above: New in 1962, this BOC Bristol SUS4A with 30-seat ECW body is in many ways the predecessor of today's midibuses.
Edward Shirras

Left: This lighter livery, using more cream, was introduced to help identify BOC's driver-only buses, like this 1965 Bristol MW5G with 45-seat ECW body seen in 1968.
J Reeves

Left: Generations of Bristol K type double-deckers served the Bristol Omnibus Company's area, with many concentrated on Bristol City services like this late-model KSW6G with 60-seat ECW body.
Ted Jones

Below: Bristol Omnibus continued to buy Bristol KSW types alongside Lodekkas until 1957. These were normal height buses for the Bristol City fleet like this 1957 example seen in 1971.
Ted Jones

Parked up at BOC's busy Lawrence Hill depot in Bristol, a rather careworn Bristol KSW from the last batch delivered, in 1957. Sausage adverts seemed to be popular on BOC buses at this time.
Tony Wilson

Right: Another of the once-ubiquitous Bristol KSWs in the Bristol Omnibus fleet, a 1955 example at Downend, Bristol. The advertisement promotes Associated Motorways coach services.
Royston Morgan

Centre: Some of the BOC KSWs lasted into the National Bus Company 'double-N' logo phase, like this slightly battered 1956 bus seen at Filton with the traditional fleetname and crest on the lower panels and the NBC logo and a corporate advert on the upper panels.
Tony Wilson

Below: The Bath Services name continued in use on a number of Bristol Omnibus vehicles after the previously separate Bath companies were wound up in 1969. This is a Bristol LS5G/ECW at Devizes in 1966.
Mark Page

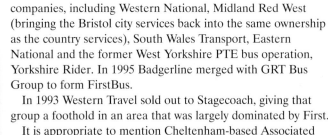

companies, including Western National, Midland Red West (bringing the Bristol city services back into the same ownership as the country services), South Wales Transport, Eastern National and the former West Yorkshire PTE bus operation, Yorkshire Rider. In 1995 Badgerline merged with GRT Bus Group to form FirstBus.

In 1993 Western Travel sold out to Stagecoach, giving that group a foothold in an area that was largely dominated by First.

It is appropriate to mention Cheltenham-based Associated Motorways, formed in 1934 to pool the operations of a number of important express coach operators including Bristol Greyhound and Royal Blue. Black & White Motorways, also based in Cheltenham, was a founder member of Associated Motorways and its substantial fleet consisted entirely of express coaches. In 1970 its 119-strong fleet was made up of AECs, Daimlers and Leylands. The company was jointly owned by Bristol Omnibus, City of Oxford and Midland Red.

Independent local bus service operators were fairly thin on the ground in 1970, but notable firms included Pulham's of Bourton-on-the-Water, running services in the Bourton, Cheltenham and Moreton-in-Marsh areas, and Cottrell's of Mitcheldean, running between Ruardean and Gloucester. ■

Above: A former dual-purpose 1965 BOC Bristol MW6G in later years at Cheltenham as a driver-only bus.
Edward Shirras

Left: Rather surprisingly, in the early 1970s Bristol Omnibus started a programme of extensive rebuilds of elderly Bristol LSs. This 1957 LS6G is seen when the rebuild was almost complete, with a new windscreen, fluorescent lighting, new interior panelling and cream window rubbers. In this form the rebuilt buses lasted until the late 1970s.

Left: The 53-seat Bristol RELL6L proved a useful vehicle for many of BOC's 'country' services. This 1967 example is in Marlborough High Street on the service to Swindon.
M Bennett

Top: In the Bristol City fleet, a 1969 Bristol RELL6L/ECW seen when new.
A R Macfarlane

Above: The lighter livery was also used with Cheltenham District maroon as a relief colour. This two-door Bristol RELL6L is seen in 1971 on a Cheltenham town service.
Edward Shirras

The Bath Services fleet also included some of the short-length Bristol SUS4A with 30-seat ECW bodywork.
Geoff Lumb

The Bristol Lodekka became BOC's standard double-decker after 1957. This LD type is seen in Swindon in November 1969.
Ted Jones

Another Lodekka working in the centre of Bristol in June 1970. And, yes – it has a sausage advert.
Tony Wilson

Top: Cheltenham District buses continued to wear this maroon and cream livery and when the main Bristol Omnibus fleet received the NBC corporate leaf green colour Cheltenham buses became NBC poppy red for a short period. This Lodekka is in the centre of Cheltenham in September 1969.
Chris Aston

Above: Parked up at Gloucester bus station in 1969, a Lodekka FLF6G and an MW5G sit in the sun waiting for their next duties.
Ted Jones

Left: In the 1960s BOC adopted the longer FLF type Lodekka, like this FLF6G seen in Cheltenham in 1972. Sausages still figure in the advertising.
Mark Page

Above: Although most of BOC's later Bristol RELL6Ls had dual-door ECW bodies, some, like this 1971 example seen in Swindon in 1971, had 50-seat one-door bodies.

A Swain

Below: In 1967 Bristol Omnibus transferred 1960/61 Bristol Lodekka FSF6Gs to Western/Southern National in exchange for FLF6G Lodekkas. In 1970 BOC took over Western National's Chippenham and Trowbridge services, along with 24 buses which included the return of the FSFs. One is seen in Chippenham in August 1970, back in the BOC fleet.

M A Penn

Above: The two 1966 Bristol VRX6G prototypes, featuring longitudinal engines, were acquired by Bristol Omnibus in 1970. This one is wearing Gloucester fleetnames in 1967.
Peter G Davey

Below: Heading out of St Margaret's Coach Station in Cheltenham bound for Weston-super-Mare in 1968, a Bristol Greyhound Bristol RELH6G/ECW coach.
Edward Shirras

Above: A Bristol RELH6G/ECW coach later in its BOC life, painted as a dual-purpose vehicle and fitted with bus-type destination display and folding door, at Swindon's old bus station in November 1969.
Ted Jones

Below: Still operating as a long-distance coach in March 1972 and wearing the Bristol Greyhound version of the south-west coach livery, a Bristol RELH6G pauses in Marlborough.
Ted Jones

Above: Leaving Chepstow on the Cardiff-Bristol service late in 1969, a Bristol RELH6L of that year with ECW flat-front deep-screen body fitted out as a dual-purpose 49-seater.
Ted Jones

Below: Similar Bristol RELH coaches from the Royal Blue and Bristol Greyhound fleets sit together at Victoria Coach Station, London.
Ted Jones

Above: Delivered late in 1970, a Bristol Greyhound-liveried Leyland Leopard PSU3A/4R with Plaxton Elite 47-seat body, seen at Reading in March 1971.

M A Penn

Below: The imposing façade of Cheltenham coach station on Boxing Day 1968, with a fine selection of Black & White AEC, Daimler and Leyland coaches, all but the Harrington-bodied vehicle on the right carrying Plaxton bodies.

Edward Shirras

Above: An impressive mid-1960s coach, a Black & White Leyland Leopard PSU3/3R with Harrington Grenadier 47-seat body, at Victoria Coach Station, London.

Below: Pulham's of Bourton-on-the-Water bought new vehicles for its main Cheltenham-Bourton service, like this Leyland Leopard/ Plaxton Elite.
Edward Shirras

Above: Cheltenham was the hub of the Associated Motorways operation and this Black & White 1963 Leyland Leopard PSU3/3R with Plaxton Panorama 47-seat body is seen in May 1969 ready to depart for Derby.
Chris Aston

Below: One of the longest-surviving bus operators in Gloucestershire is Pulham of Bourton-on-the-Water, whose Ford R192/Plaxton bus is seen in Cheltenham in October 1970.
Chris Aston